DESKTOP DOG PARKS

A Field Guide

T0364049

Running Press
Hachette Book Group
1290 Avenue of the Americas, New York, NY 10104
www.runningpress.com
@Running_Press

First Edition: October 2018

Published by Running Press, an imprint of Perseus Books, LLC, a subsidiary of Hachette Book Group, I The Running Press name and logo is a trademark o the Hachette Book Group.

The publisher is not responsible for websites (or th content) that are not owned by the publisher.

ISBN: 978-0-7624-6484-5

CONTENTS

DESKTOP DOG PARKS:

an introduction

10 out of 10 dogs agree: Dog parks are the freaking best! A dedicated place to pee, sniff other dogs' butts, and roll in mud—all without angering the humans? Heck yes!

And while nothing quite compares to the experience of taking Fido to the park and letting him go buck wild, sometimes you just can't get over to the dog park with your pup. If you're stuck at work and missing your pooch and his pals, or you're longing for a four-legged companion but aren't sure you can handle the commitment, you're in luck. This tiny *Desktop Dog Park* is the perfect way to create a clean, hassle- and odor-free canine oasis right on your desk (or any surface in need of some puppy love). We hope this replica of the real thing offers you a bout of anytime animal therapy.

DESKTOP DOG PARKS:
a field guide

You and your pooch might know your way around a "real" dog park, but there's lots to learn about desktop dog parks and their unique customs and cast of characters.

THE LINGO

- **Pup, pupper, puppo, pooch, doggo, doggie, woofer:**
  A dog. We'll use these terms interchangeably throughout to refer to man's best friend.

- **Wagger:**
  Can refer to a dog itself, or his happily wagging tail.

- **Snoot:**
  A.k.a. snout, schnozz, sniffer —a dog's nose.

Whosagooddog:

A common human-to-dog greeting. Other variations include
"whosagoodboy," common for
greeting male dogs; "whosa-
goodgirl" for female pups; and
"whosapuppy," which can be
used to greet both adult dogs
and puppies.

THE PARK

This dog-park-in-a-box is a snap to assemble. You'll be enjoying your pup paradise in no time at all Dump out the contents of the box and you'll find:

A) 5 tiny resin dogs
of various breeds (more on those breeds starting on page 18!), all house-trained, quiet, and extremely well behaved

B) 1 fire hydrant
(for when nature calls)

C) A plush felt lawn
to set the scene and keep your
pups contained

A

B

C

SETTING UP YOUR PARK

Go ahead and scout your desk for the perfect dog park location. May we suggest by the phone, so your doggos can keep you company on every conference call? Or maybe in your inbox, to let people know you are not interested in their memos and that your dogs are the only responsibility you need today? The possibilities are endless, but any flat surface will do.

----

ay the lawn down first. Bam—park created. Those dogs aren't going anywhere! Set your fire hydrant somewhere all the pooches can clearly see it so you don't have any messes on your hands. Then, let your dogs out and let the fun begin!

THE DOGS

Now the moment you've all been waiting for—let's meet those canines! While the crew of dogs varies from park to park, you'll typically see at least one or two of these types on any given day. The five breeds herein are common denizens of life-size dog parks, and the characters included in the *Desktop Dog Park* all have distinct personalities that will make for some interesting interactions.

DASH THE DACHSHUND

Nicknames: Longboy, Noodle, Stretch

Appearance: Chestnut coat; brigh and alert face; squat legs; *looong* back and snoot

Behavior: Dash is a sweet boy with a BIG personality—much bigger than his low-lying stature might suggest. What he lacks in height he makes up for in gumption and length, of course): He'll sniff your pup's butt whether it's a big ol' barker or a tiny l'il pipsqueak. His rodent-like body makes him a great burrower and digger. He also hates the rain, so you might find him hiding under Rosie during storms at the park.

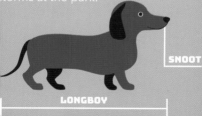

SNOOT

LONGBOY

GOOD GIRL

SIDEKICK

MAXINE THE LABRADOR

Nicknames: Maxie, Pretty Girl

Appearance: Silky golden coat; happy smiling face; wagging tail, always (even in her sleep)

Behavior: Maxine is a big goofy girl that loves fetching tennis balls and doing whatever makes her human happy. She's on the larger side, but her smiling, panting face and perpetually wagging tail make it clear she's a gentle giant incapable of hurting a fly. She gets along with all of her desktop dog park companions, though she is a bit wary of Dash and his intrusive snoot.

BEAN THE POMERANIAN

LITTLE GIRL

BIG PERSONALITY

Nicknames: Beanie Baby, Floofmonster

Appearance: Extremely fluffy light brown coat with white patches; tiny frame; perky ears and tail; always-happy face

Behavior: Bean is the princess of the bunch. Like most small dogs, she seems to compensate for her size with a large personality, one that commands attention. Her sassiness is complemented, though, by her affinity for cuddles and snoozing with both humans and other puppos. You'll usually find her hanging out with Rosie, since Bean thinks they're the same size. She's more of a lounger than a ball-chaser, though she'll occasionally have a bout of energy and want to run with the big dogs.

SHINY COAT

GENTLE GIANT

ROSIE THE ROTTWEILER

Nicknames: Sweetie, Killer, Agent Black

Appearance: Shiny black and brown coat; intimidating presence but sweet eyes and wiggly little tail

Behavior: Don't let Rosie's strong, stocky build fool you—she is a total sweetheart! Her demeanor is almost bashful, having spent her life trying to convince people she's not a killing machine. She loves running laps around the park, chasing tennis balls, and serving as a body guard for her friends (of the human and canine variety).

RILO THE CORGI

Nicknames: Floofy Butt, Chunks, Snickers

Appearance: Short and long like Dash, but with some extra meat and fluff on the frame; fox-like ears; adorable fluffy butt and a happy little tail

Behavior: Few things are cuter than a Corgi butt, and Rilo knows it—this pup is confident, crafty, and knows how to get a treat out of any situation. His affinity for peanut

utter and his candy-like shape
and color have earned him the
nickname "Snickers," along with
others he's less than enthused
about. He plays well with other
dogs but also loves hanging out
on his own (with a toy filled with
peanut butter, that is).

BONE

FLUFFY
BUTT